Unconventional Warfare 2.0

A Better Path to Regime Change in the Twenty First Century

Christopher Rawley

Unconventional Warfare 2.0: A Better Path to Regime Change in the Twenty First
Century
Christopher Rawley

1. unconventional warfare 2. regime change 3. revolution 4. insurgency 5. War 6.
Special operations 7. subversion

Third Edition

Cover photo: Libyan government fighters celebrate after seizing the stronghold of
Gaddafi in Bani Walid in 2011. Creative Commons license by Essam Mohamed

☐ ISBN-10: 149928232X
ISBN-13: 978-1499282320

CONTENTS

"Liberty, when it begins to take root, is a plant of rapid growth." – George Washington

1 INTRODUCTION

A rapidly evolving geopolitical environment and fiscal necessity are driving America's security policy to a new strategic crossroads. As military forces draw down from protracted, costly counterinsurgency campaigns, the U.S. and other industrialized nations must make decisions on future force capabilities in order to optimize decreasing military budgets and limited end strength while dealing with continuing threats. Force reductions are an inevitable outcome of war conclusion, and involve trade-offs between service capabilities. Budget considerations normally include readiness, force end-strength, the fate of acquisition programs, and research and development. Generally, these choices take future threats into account although they can be heavily influenced by recent war-time experiences.

Across the spectrum of threats, rogue regimes present a frequently recurring challenge to U.S. national security. These governments threaten regional stability, often seek weapons of mass destruction as deterrence, may sponsor terrorist proxies, and more often than not, violently repress their populations. Military history is replete with conflicts and diplomatic stand-offs involving authoritarian leaders. Infamous characters such as Hitler, Stalin, Castro, Hussein, Gadhafi, Assad, and the Kim dynasty have extracted an inordinate amount of energy, blood, and treasure from the world's militaries and diplomats in the past century. A variety of tools of statecraft are available for policy makers to deal with these states, ranging from sanctions and diplomacy, to punitive strikes and raids, to the most severe option – outright regime change.

Regime change is the process by which a state removes an offensive regime – by any number of means – and replaces it with a less offensive one.[1] Several times in its history, the U.S. has chosen to implement regime change in response to these onerous and illegitimate governments. In some cases, such as in Germany and Iraq, the U.S. military waged major conventional war and subsequent occupation to affect regime change. Other campaigns to remove an incumbent belligerent government involved covert activities. While still others employed more overt use of ground-based surrogates supported by various U.S. military capabilities such as special operations and airpower. Afghanistan in 2001 and Libya in 2011 were examples of the latter approach.

These campaigns, sometimes referred to as unconventional warfare (UW), enable elements of disgruntled populations to overthrow the regime in power. Contrast these efforts to Iraq in 2003, where a swift conventional military invasion by hundreds of thousands of troops succeeded in rapidly deposing the regime, but the follow on occupying ground force was then unable to maintain order and prevent a subsequent insurgency against the nascent Iraqi government.

An integrated UW campaign is a worthwhile approach when regime change is chosen as a national policy option. Consequently, the United States and its allies must evolve and enhance joint and interagency capabilities to support these campaigns.

2 UNCONVENTIONAL WARFARE AS A STRATEGY

"The few active rebels must have the qualities of speed and endurance, ubiquity and independence of arteries of supply. They must have the technical equipment to destroy or paralyze the enemy's organized communications." – T.E. Lawrence, **The Science of Guerrilla Warfare**

The United States military's doctrinal definition of UW has evolved over the years, with revisions articulated in 1951, 1961, 1967, 1969, and 1988. Earlier versions emphasized the indirect military objectives of harassing, delaying and disrupting military operations of the enemy with irregular or partisan forces, often in conjunction with a broader war effort.[2] The doctrine was most recently revised in 2009 by the commanders of United States Special Operations Command and Army Special Operations Command to read: "Unconventional Warfare consists of activities conducted to enable a resistance movement or insurgency to coerce, disrupt or overthrow an occupying power or government by operating through or with an underground, auxiliary and guerrilla force in a denied area."[3] UW activities may include support to insurgent sabotage and subversion efforts. Sabotage will normally focus on attacking regime centers of gravities, including both military nodes and economic infrastructure, such as petroleum facilities. These attacks usually take the form of bombings, kidnappings, and assassinations. The improvised explosive device, or IED, has become the weapon of choice by today's insurgents, for whom other heavy weaponry is often unavailable. IEDs of increasing sophistication continue to proliferate in insurgencies across Africa, the Levant, and Central Asia and bomb-making instructions can be found all over the Internet. Subversive activities take many forms and are designed to destabilize and discredit a hostile regime. During the Cold War, British and U.S. secret services implemented a variety of subversion techniques to designed ridicule and undermine the Soviet Union. Subversive messaging is often also used to manipulate ethnic tensions. Today, much of this messaging takes place in cyberspace, which will be discussed in more detail later.

Although the tactic of UW does not always have a goal of regime replacement, the doctrinal evolution towards more strategic objectives – including overthrowing governments – may be reflective of more recent military experiences where half-measures did not achieve policy goals. Large scale invasions and occupations are becoming less viable as a means of regime change for several reasons. First, U.S. Army and Marine Corps force structure is being drawn down to such a point to make future interventions of this magnitude difficult, if not impossible to accomplish. Second, as Richard Haas argues, "the rise of nationalism, together with globalization (and the increased availability of powerful means of resistance), may have doomed prolonged occupations of foreign countries by sharply increasing their human, military, and economic cost."[4] Another factor against these sorts of military incursions is a globally-instantaneous continuous media cycle that tends to play to the side of the defending regime. UW may be appropriate when a major conventional military campaign is politically unpalatable, either domestically or in the view of the international community. In 2011, echoing General MacArthur, Secretary of Defense Robert Gates bluntly reflected that reality when he said, "any future defense secretary who advises the president to again send a big American land army into Asia or into the Middle East or Africa 'should have his head examined.'"

An UW campaign may be the method of choice when general purpose forces are not available in the numbers required to conduct a conventional invasion, or the lines of communication are too long to support the logistics required for a large ground presence, as was the case during the initial stages of Operation Enduring Freedom in Afghanistan. UW campaigns are also significantly less costly than a ground invasion, requiring much smaller numbers of troops, logistics, and equipment. Purely from a financial standpoint to the countries involved, a UW campaign can be a bargain compared to the conventional alternative. For example, the regime change operation in Libya cost the United States approximately $1 billion and took about seven months. In Iraq, about $100 billion was spent by U.S. taxpayers on the initial invasion and occupation until the time Saddam Hussein was captured in December 2013. That cost obviously doesn't include the next seven years of counterinsurgency and rebuilding, which ran into the trillions of dollars by some estimates.

While troop requirements may be quite small on the part of the unit executing the UW operation, supported guerrilla forces can develop into large scale military formations. Insurgencies are not limited by the usual constraints on military manpower. Volunteer fighters, both native and from abroad, live off the land, and do not require large infrastructures to house and feed them. Whereas professional militaries are bound by international restrictions on child soldiers, children are a common occurrence on insurgent manpower. Women and the elderly also fill out the troop formations of revolutions, whether as fighters, or auxiliary. Meanwhile, small teams executing UW leverage the insurgents' logistics tails.

The leveraged power of a small UW footprint was demonstrated during World War II in the China-Burma-India Theater, where the U.S. Office of Strategic Services' Det 101 supported Kachin Rangers which eventually became a conventional force of 10,000 troops.[5] Finally, as America's intervention with NATO in Libya demonstrated, UW campaigns are compatible with coalition warfare, with different nations contributing different capabilities along with their own national caveats on how their troops can be employed. Some countries may choose to send in special operations forces to advise insurgents (as the Qataris did in Libya), while others may just support an air campaign (as the United States and other allies did).

Certain conditions lend themselves to an unconventional warfare campaign versus other forms of regime change. First, a state's power should be concentrated in the hands of a relatively small number of individuals who are unresponsive to the population. An UW campaign would be unlikely to work against a representative democracy where power is dispersed throughout the state in viable executive, judicial, and parliamentary institutions at various levels of government. Second, large scale popular dissatisfaction with the ruling government should be present, even if that dissatisfaction has been suppressed or is latent. The rapid overthrow of Mubarak's regime in Egypt in 2011 was the result of a long standing, latent popular revolution. Other "Arab Spring" revolutions resulted from similar pent up frustration with ineffective and governments.

The Economist Intelligence Unit's "Index of Democracy" provides a tool which might be useful in assessing some of the indicators which can make a regime conducive to replacement via UW.[6] Low measures of pluralism, political participation, and civil liberties are indicative of a country with potential for revolution. Clearly, a deeper study of the political and social dynamics inherent in contemporary revolution is warranted, but some nations that might currently fit these criteria include Iran, China, Syria, Eritrea, and Myanmar. These countries diverge from North Korea in that the population there has been severely indoctrinated over multiple generations, and the latent dissatisfaction has given way to resignation and acquiescence, if not outright devotion to the highly repressive regime.[7] Finally, as we shall see, UW is not the sole purview of nation states, and it is increasingly common for non-state actors to participate in these operations.

3 EVOLVING INSURGENCIES AND UW

"Tomorrow is Egyptians' day of anger. We will make noise in the streets of all major Egyptian cities. This will be a peaceful protest against torture and humiliation that Egyptians face inside their own country. We will make noise to show our discontent to the election fraud that happens in every election and which is due to happen in the next elections on Sunday 28th. Are you supporting us?" – 25 November 2010 entry on the "We are all Khaled Said" Facebook page

Understanding how an insurgency works is a key to crafting a successful UW campaign. Although all insurgencies throughout history share similar profiles, globalization, mobile technology, and changing demographics have impacted the modern revolution. Traditional UW doctrine states that an insurgency is broken into three components: 1) the underground primarily collects intelligence in support of the movement; 2) the auxiliary provides logistical and other support to the resistance movement; and 3) guerrilla fighters serve as the action arm of any insurgency movement.[8]

The traditional definitions of underground, auxiliary, and guerrilla force may no longer appropriate in all cases of revolution. Recent mass, persistent protest movements do not necessarily reflect this model and seem to work by bringing international opinion to bear against the government in power. In Egypt, for example, change didn't require guerrilla fighters or supporting underground and auxiliary forces. Instead, mass protests televised live across the world drove the military to replace Mubarak in lieu of allowing the significant public blood shed that would have been required to suppress the protests. In 2011, Tunisian protesters who had formerly relied on a resistance organization based around union committees, realized that the absence of a centralized command and general chaos in the ongoing revolution hindered a more structured response by regime security forces. As one might expect, a decentralized organization had more initiative and was more agile. Government elements supporting such a resistance movement should take these dynamics into account.

Much like a self-organizing criminal "flash mob," these sorts of rapid regime changes might best be characterized as a "flash insurgency," and are distinct from protracted rural insurgencies. Examples of urban-based regime changes that occurred relatively quickly include the French Revolution (1871), the Bolshevik Revolution (1917), Bolivia in 1952, and Iran in 1978-79.[9] In some cases, a catalyzing event precipitates these revolutions, such as the self-immolation of a vegetable vendor over high food prices in Tunisia that kick started uprisings across North Africa and the Middle East. The 2011 "Arab Spring" revolutions were typical of these rapid regime changes, although some of these mass revolts were tamped down, at least initially, by the ruling regime, including those in Syria, Saudi Arabia, and Bahrain. Libyan revolutionaries may have suffered a similar fate had NATO not intervened. NATO offensive military operations in Libya began as an effort to protect the people from the regime, but after some months evolved into a semi-cohesive UW campaign. Some of these recent revolutions have been violent, but others, such as Egypt, occurred with relatively minimal fighting between the incumbent state and the revolutionaries. Urban insurgencies can be quickly crushed by the application of massive violence, but "even when a state has high capacity for organized violence, it can *choose* to avoid embracing this option."[10] To wit, 846 people were reported killed over the course of 18 days of protests in Egypt, which, although not an insignificant loss of life, pales in comparison to the death tolls usually accommodating prolonged civil wars.[11] As a point of comparison, the United Nations estimates that as of early 2014, more than 150,000 people had been killed and four million displaced in Syria's civil war.

UW as a tool for regime change has several drawbacks. As we discovered in Iraq and Afghanistan, *regime replacement* is often more difficult than regime removal.[12] For example, America's lack of understanding of the players after the Taliban were removed from power in Afghanistan drove unwise support to certain political candidates, the development of a constitution that didn't recognize traditional forms of patronage, and a favoring of the Pashtuns over other ethnic groups including the Uzbeks, Hazars and Tajiks who had contributed more to the collapse of the Taliban government.[13] These poor decisions continue to drive the illegitimacy of the current government there and fuel the ongoing insurgency. Post-conflict problems may occur though, regardless of how regime change is implemented, as the Iraq conventional invasion and subsequent occupation painfully demonstrated. One advantage of UW is that by teaming with the population actually overthrowing the incumbent government, the external power is able to better understand the political dynamics, and is not left "holding the bag" alone once the regime falls, as happened in Iraq.

Early on in the development of UW doctrine, the necessity of a solid population-centric focus was recognized: "If the U.S. is to work successfully through a local people, it is essential that an understanding concerning how that society functions be developed on the part of our personnel involved, to enable them to anticipate correctly the results of actions they plan to take."[14]

A firm understanding of the cultural and political landscape is even more important today, as globalization and democracy overlaid with tribal and sectarian societies makes for an extremely complex political dynamic. This condition is prominent across the Middle East and Africa and exacerbates post-revolution instability. In the case of Libya, the country quickly transitioned from one tribe running the country to more than 200 tribes attempting to exert power, but no one really in charge. The exploitation of sectarian rifts is an old tactic in the playbook of authoritarian regimes. Throughout its reign, the Assad government has adeptly labeled oppositionists as Islamists and reportedly released large numbers of Salafist criminals early in the civil war to fracture the insurgency. The Kingdom of Saudi Arabia has also used propaganda to characterize opposition movements along the Sunni-Shia rift, although more recent protests there have been more broad-based and secular.

A second risk is that influencing a regime change via UW has the potential to result in long standing animosity towards the third party interventionist. For example, the United States Central Intelligence Agency (CIA) and British Intelligence coordinated a covert UW campaign to overthrow Iran's Prime Minister in 1953, and even today, U.S. involvement in the situation remains in the memory of the Iranian people and part of the current government's propaganda.[15] On the other hand, French military support to the colonists in America's own revolution contributed to one of the most successful outcomes of foreign interventions in history. The legitimacy of a replacement government will always be an issue, but a new government will likely be perceived as more legitimate if supported by large segments of the population that would be mobilized in an UW effort. Additionally, UW campaigns can be overt, clandestine, or covert, so a degree of non-attribution may actually be possible for the intervening parties.

Although an actual regime might fall quite rapidly upon the initiation of hostilities, UW campaigns generally require long term planning and follow through. Intelligence preparation of the environment to identify appropriate surrogate partners takes time. One of the most important considerations in a UW campaign is the vetting of the insurgent forces to ensure their interests and ours are consistent. Competing political or extremist organizations may not have the same goals as the country executing an UW campaign, as was the case with al Qaeda elements aligned with some Libyan militia groups. Furthermore, failure to adequately support an insurgent movement has historically resulted in an unsuccessful regime change campaign. Examples of UW campaigns that were not sufficiently supported include the failed Bay of Pigs invasion in Cuba and clandestine efforts to assist Kurdish populations in Northern Iraq in their struggle against Saddam Hussein following Operation Desert Storm. Therefore, once the policy decision is made to conduct an UW campaign; the U.S. government must apply all instruments of national power in support of the rebelling population until the regime is displaced.

4 IMPROVING JOINT AND INTERAGENCY UW CAPABILITIES

"The problems we face in the world are not problems that come and fit neatly into one department or agency, they're problems that inevitably require the involvement and engagement of more than one department or agency and we end up spending incredible amounts of time that just kind of suck the life out of you..." – **Donald Rumsfeld**

UW is a mission where interagency synchronization is absolutely critical. So-called "whole-of-government" or interagency approaches have been applied to national security problems with varying levels of success the past decade, but the involvement of non-military U.S. agencies in UW dates back to at least the 1840s campaign in Mexico. Irregulars played a part on both sides during the Mexican-American war. Prior to the war, Northern Mexico faced an Indian insurrection, primarily from Comanches and Kiowas. Despite the history of animosity between the Texas Rangers and Plains Indians, the Rangers sometimes aligned themselves with Indians against the Mexican military. More recently, the efficacy of interagency support to counter-insurgency efforts in Iraq and Afghanistan is worthy of debate. Much of the promised non-military contributions to these campaigns in the form of civilian boots-on-the-ground did not fully materialize. On the other hand, after some fits and starts, the coordination between DOD, intelligence services, and law enforcement agencies in the global campaign against al Qaeda appears to be a notable success.

UW has been a cornerstone mission for United States Army Special Forces (SF) since the first Special Forces Group was created in 1952.[16] The heart of the SF organization is a 12-man Operational Detachment Alpha, or "ODA." These teams are cross-trained in a variety of specialties including weapons, engineering, communications, and medicine. In addition to performing various light infantry tasks and direct action missions, ODAs are adept at linking up with, training, and supporting indigenous forces, including insurgent movements.

SF and CIA personnel have cooperated closely in UW campaigns in order to maximize the authorities and skills of the respective organizations. Army SF's training and selection process includes exercises where soldiers learn to connect with and support rural guerrillas. This training has served SF well throughout their history as was demonstrated brilliantly during the initial UW campaign in Afghanistan in 2001. However, the capabilities required to transform rural *campesinos* into a guerrilla army are dissimilar from those needed to foment and support an insurgency among highly urbanized and educated populations. Several factors inherent in Twenty-First Century insurgencies require new approaches to UW.

Demographic trends will drive new conflict and newer ways of fighting. By 2050, there will be over 9 billion people on earth. Much of this rapid growth will continue in less-developed regions of the world, with the "youth bulge" more prominent in the Middle East and Africa. Urbanization of the world's population appears to be an unstoppable force; therefore SF should train to facilitate insurgencies in an urban environment. Urban terrain adds layers of complexity to all types of warfare to include insurgencies. Urbanization brings with it higher rates of crime, pollution, and sprawling slums. Large cities have traditionally been viewed as inhospitable to insurgencies "because their atomistic nature makes betrayal more likely, their populations are not fertile territory for identity-based political mobilization, and cities smaller in size [in relation to rural areas] allows government forces to easily control them."[17] Conversely, built up cities can degrade high-technology weapons, intelligence, and communications, and present higher opportunities for collateral damage. During Arab Spring protests, opposition leaders made urban working-class neighborhoods a key focus of their campaigns. This strategy ensured that the movements were seen as broad-based, and not simply tied to intelligentsia in exile. While these factors pose a challenge to the counter-insurgent, they can be leveraged to the advantage of the insurgent and supporting UW advisors.[18]

Second, UW operations don't always require boots on the ground. Conceivably, a "virtual UW" campaign can be waged, with financial, intelligence, and propaganda support being provided remotely to insurgents. Training of surrogate forces can also take place in a nearby third country. SF teams conducting UW normally deploy to austere locations and are effective in part because their team leaders have the freedom to improvise and quickly make decisions at the local level. In a virtual UW campaign, commanders may be tempted to centralize planning, but in order facilitate speedy decision making, authorities should be appropriately delegated. Employing other agencies' authorities is another way that this speed of action can be maintained. For example, in certain circumstances law enforcement and other government agencies' authorities to engage in cyber-activities may be authorized at lower levels than the Department of Defense (DOD) allows. Cyber-authorities to conduct information operations must be more freely employed by other agencies and coordinated with, if not directed by, DOD. Along these lines, U.S. Cyber Command should work with U.S. Special Operations Command and other agencies to incorporate support to UW campaigns into the cyber-portfolio. Future UW doctrine should also consider the use of smaller virtual planning teams (regardless of their location) with delegated authority to act as they see fit.

Overt and covert financing have been traditional means of supporting revolutions. In Afghanistan for example, SF and CIA teams flew in carrying large sums of cash to fund Northern Alliance fighters and other warlords fighting to depose the Taliban. Today, there are numerous alternatives to cash payments, and some of them are more easily targeted and disbursed. Electronic mobile money systems and traditional *hawala* dealers are exploited by criminal and terror networks to move illicitly gained money, but they could also be used in UW operations to clandestinely fund opposition movements. In addition to supporting the insurgents, UW campaigns can also block the offending regime's access to financial assets. The U.S. Treasury Department has a role to play in UW in conjunction with DOD and international partners to identify key regime targets for designation by the Office of Foreign Asset Control and United Nations. For example, in 2011 the Treasury Department froze $30 billion of Muammar Gadhafi's government and personal assets.[19]

Next, efforts to influence the population, the incumbent regime, and international opinion are an integral part of any insurgency campaign. People and financial sectors are increasingly linked together globally with networks, cell phones, and satellite communications. Whereas previously the connectivity these technologies provide were resident only in militaries, today they provide constant global reach to anyone, anywhere. Moreover, the saturation of modern mobile communications and the Internet have liberated information, even to uneducated segments of population. This information can be manipulated by UW practitioners to support the insurgents while countering the incumbent regime's narratives and censorship. Forces involved in UW must understand how a latent insurgency transitions into a flash insurgency and how to precipitate this sort of transition.

> The will to revolt, so widespread as to be almost universal today, seems to be something more than a reaction to political circumstances or material conditions. What it seems to express is a newly awakened consciousness, not of "causes" but of potentiality…The effect of this sudden awareness, this sudden fruition of consciousness, is to produce in the so-called backward areas of the world, all at once, a pervasive and urgent desire for radical change, based on new insight, startling in its simplicity, that the conditions of life that had seemed immutable can, after all, be changed.[20]

UW practitioners therefore require the ability to develop and transmit simple thematic messaging to create a mass "fruition of consciousness" and the impetus for regime change. Accordingly, Special Forces should become knowledgeable in non-military electronic communications and cyber-security techniques or integrate non-SF specialists – either military or from other agencies – with these skills into their teams. Anti-regime propaganda and messages to sway the population towards revolution can be developed by Military Information Support Operations (commonly referred to as psychological operations) soldiers or other agencies.

The necessity of preparations to execute the non-military aspect of UW cannot be over-emphasized. In the introduction to Mao Tse-Tung's *On Guerrilla Warfare*, Brigadier General S.B. Griffith, USMC, notes that "A revolutionary war is never confined within the bounds of military action. Because its purpose is to destroy an existing society and its institutions and replace them with a completely new state structure, any revolutionary war is a unity of which the constituent parts, in varying importance, are military, political, economic, social, and psychological." Accordingly, despite the challenges associated with bringing together the interagency, UW planning and execution should be inclusive.

5 EMERGING TECHNOLOGIES, TACTICS, AND PARTNERS

"The Syrian government has been monitoring (the Internet) for years. They have been using the Internet with Iranian assistance to track opposition activists, arrest and kill them."
– **Robert Ford, former U.S. ambassador to Syria**

To communicate on the urbanized, globally-networked battlefield, UW specialists must understand and develop the tools of mobile messaging, IP-based communications, and social media. These tools can be exploited to both enable the population against the regime and disrupt the regime's counter-insurgency efforts. Social media is a powerful tool for today's revolutionist. Historically, chronicling a revolution was the work of intrepid dissidents or journalists who took great risks to smuggle their writing and photographs past government censors. Today, every protestor with a mobile phone can instantly transmit sights and sounds of an ongoing revolution to world-wide audiences who follow a particular hashtag.

Intelligence preparation of the environment will determine the level of proliferation of various types of social media in the populations of interest. In Egypt in 2011, and more recently in Syria, social media was used to organize mass protests.[21] Revolutionaries there have even developed an iPhone application which "includes recent news about opposition groups and their activities, as well as videos, maps and photos."[22] Other online tools such as YouTube have been valuable in getting first-hand accounts out of the conflict zone and countering regime propaganda. U.S. Special Forces officer Lieutenant Colonel Brian Petit contends that social media supports "borderless social mobilization" and can help UW practitioners to shape the digital narrative.[23] Developing these narratives requires a strong understanding of the nuances of language, culture, and history. Because military forces are rotational, they should work with civilian and academic experts who have more in-depth experience in the particular country of interest.

Tradecraft is a term used by intelligence agencies that refers to methods of espionage and human intelligence collection. Traditional methods of tradecraft, such as the "dead drop" to exchange messages clandestinely still occur, but are rapidly being replaced by digital tradecraft techniques. Intelligence analysis in support of digital tradecraft begins by establishing the extent of government monitoring, censoring, and restrictions on Internet and social media access. UW forces can help rebels establish communications secure from regime surveillance by organizing dark networks, or darknets. One example of current darknets is peer-to-peer gaming systems which have been used by drug trafficking organizations to communicate clandestinely.[24] Another way that insurgents, terrorists, and narco-traffickers talk to one another is by encrypting their Internet-based communications with a tool called Tor. A limitation of Tor is that individual data packets can be tracked and therefore blocked by government censors in informationally-restricted countries such as Iran and China. A software tool called SkypeMorph has been developed which camouflages Tor communications as Skype packets which enable darknets to overcome censors that are hesitant to block other forms of Internet traffic. UW forces should understand the employment of a wide variety of these ever-changing tools. Electromagnetically dense urban centers are another area where UW forces could assist insurgents in developing secure underground darknets using Wi-Fi technology to create peer-to-peer router networks. In addition to security, digital tradecraft can facilitate the entire range of sabotage and subversion in a UW campaign.

SF has always been adept at working with traditional guerrilla fighters, underground, and auxiliary forces, but future UW operations will require engagement with new types of surrogates. The "digital underground" is usually decentralized, self-forming, and cellular.[25] Another variation of these actors are cyber vigilantes, who may or may not be part of the rebelling population. Recent revolutions have seen digital undergrounds composed of various combinations students, soccer hooligans, diaspora activists, and anonymous collectives of computer experts. During the Arab Spring uprisings, an international hacker group known as Telecomix took over Internet users' browsers in Syria and replaced them with instructions on how to use free encryption and anonymity software to evade government censorship and surveillance. Telecomix also published Internet proxy logs from a United States company which was inadvertently helping the Syrian regime to spy on its citizens' web usage, a potential violation of international sanctions.[26] These vigilantes can be harnessed – either wittingly or unwittingly – by government entities involved in UW campaigns to perform subversive activities against incumbent regimes.

A relatively peaceful regime change should be the goal of any UW campaign, but when that is not possible, operations that enable insurgents to violently overthrow the regime may be undertaken. Although it is sometimes necessary in UW for an external actor to provide lethal aid to rebels, there are also ways to increase the opposition's lethality without directly shipping arms and munitions. Terrorist groups use the Internet to disseminate tactics and designs for improvised explosive devices and SF could likewise enable insurgents remotely by providing them advice and direction for increasing the lethality of their attacks against government security forces. Non-lethal assistance, such as medical and communications training, can also be supplied remotely.

When physical material support must be provided to rebels, UW forces should consider using existing criminal ground, air, and sea smuggling routes and methods. Illicit rat lines and gray arms networks will naturally emerge to meet insurgent demand and can be co-opted as a clandestine method of logistics support to opposition movements. Ironically, those agencies who routinely combat these types of illicit smuggling networks—including the Drug Enforcement

Agency and Immigrations and Customs Enforcement—are the ones best positioned to provide intelligence on their locations and mechanics to the interagency UW team. The types of armaments in highest demands on today's revolutionary battlefields include anti-armor and anti-aircraft weapons. These weapons are generally only available from nation states, though the fall of the Gaddafi regime led to massive stockpiles of advanced weaponry onto the black market, including shoulder-fired anti-aircraft weapons.

6 ESCALATING THE CAMPAIGN WITH AIR AND SEA POWER

"He who commands the sea has command of everything." –
Themistocles

When a virtual UW campaign is not sufficient to overthrow a regime, a more direct approach will generally entail the infiltration of combat advisors and addition of joint fire support in order to erode the regime's combat strength and centers of gravity. Both general purpose and special operations airpower capabilities can aid an UW campaign with low visibility insertion and extraction of special operations forces, and by providing precision fires and logistics in support of guerrilla fighters. Prime historical examples of these campaigns included the aerial resupply missions flown in support of the French resistance in World War II and CIA "Air America" and US Air Force commando flights supporting Hmong guerrillas in Laos in the 1960s.[27] These UW operations drove the innovative tactics and equipment developments reflected in today's Air Force Special Operations Command. Another more recent example of the effectiveness of air power in UW was demonstrated when Kurdish *Peshmerga* rebels and their U.S. SF advisors, aided by U.S. Navy and Air Force close air support, pinned down 12 of Iraq's 20 divisions in Northern Iraq, preventing their movement to reinforce the conventional invasion in the south.[28] Modern airpower is devastating to armor and can provide over-matched insurgents protection from superior regime ground forces.

An intermediate step to offensive air operations is the imposition of a "no-fly zone," which can mitigate the risk of the regime's own airpower on insurgent forces. Rebel ground forces, even those possessing rudimentary armor, are easily overmatched by a regime's tactical fixed wing or helicopter gun-ships. A no-fly-zone campaign usually consist of an initial suppression of enemy air defenses (SEAD) by bombing or missiles to safeguard friendly aircraft, then maintenance of no-fly areas with combat air patrols and additional SEAD as required. No fly zones can also be supported with theater surface-to-air missiles, such as the Patriot, deployed just outside a country's borders. Long duration no-fly zones during the 1990s prevented Saddam Hussein from bombing his own rebelling populations in northern and southern Iraq, but were not tied to complementary ground efforts to produce more decisive effects.

A lower-cost, though in some ways, higher-risk alternative to establishing a no-fly zone is to supply surrogate forces with anti-aircraft missiles. Portable, fire-and-forget shoulder-launched anti-aircraft missiles, sometimes referred to as man-portable air defense systems, or MANPADS, provide a guerrilla force with the means to resist a regime's airpower. Although not necessarily effective against high flying modern jet tactical aircraft equipped with counter-measures, MANPADs can increase the risk to the regime's lower flying aircraft, especially helicopters. Beginning in 1986, the United States supplied *Mujadin* fighters operating in Afghanistan with infrared-guided Stinger missiles, a program so successful that it likely turned the tide against the Soviets there. Thereafter, accountability for hundreds of these missiles was lost as they dispersed all over Central Asia. MANPADs are regarded as especially dangerous in the hands of terrorist groups for their potential to shoot down commercial aircraft. Following the Soviet withdrawal, the United States spent millions of dollars and nearly two decades trying to account for and buy-back the missing missiles. Despite the likely impact MANPADs could make to a rebel force, based on the fall-out from Pakistan, there is a significant hesitation on the part of modern militaries to equip rebel armies with these potent weapons.

With the advent of unmanned airborne intelligence, surveillance, and reconnaissance (ISR) platforms, intelligence on regime force disposition and intentions can be shared with insurgents without risking coalition aviators over contested air space. In some cases, intelligence support could be done without direct U.S. ground presence by providing real time ISR video feeds directly to the rebels. Today's foreign disclosure processes are often clumsy and slow, so mechanisms to provide real time intelligence to opposition movements without violating operational security or revealing sensitive technology should be developed. As an alternative to injecting more armaments into a volatile environment, rebels could also be supplied with small, tactical unmanned aerial vehicles as an affordable means for organic ISR. Insurgents and terrorist have been known to access Google Earth satellite imagery for targeting. Additionally, the advent of commercially-available "drones" and quad-rotors brings the potential for real time airborne video feed to insurgents for just a few hundred dollars. The Internet promulgates best practices for airborne surveillance across insurgencies.

Despite its value, airpower in UW campaigns comes with caveats. First, the availability of ground forces to direct fires from the air or sea will produce more precise and effective results. These forces can be U.S. or coalition special operators; or, if properly trained and equipped, even the guerrillas themselves. Second, the use of friendly ground forces generally assumes that the coalition has air superiority over the regime's military. The risk to SF combat advisors working with surrogates significantly increases if they are under threat from air attack by regime forces. Conversely, built up, highly populated urban terrain can be a hindrance to employing fires from the air due to collateral damage considerations. These considerations can also favor the insurgents, unless the regime has made a calculated decision to employ maximum firepower to suppress opposition movements in a city. Long-range precision missile fires, such as those from the Army's High Mobility Artillery Rocket System (HIMARS), could supply another way to support insurgents on the ground from over-the-horizon without risking the lives of allied aviators.

Another demographic trend related to urbanization that will define requirements for future UW campaigns is the emergence of

Mega-cities (those with more than 10 million people), which appear mostly in coastal regions. Poverty-stricken mega-cities in littoral areas such as Mumbai, Karachi, Dhaka, and Lagos are growing the fastest. Accordingly, seapower will likely play a supporting role in many future UW efforts. During Operation Odyssey Dawn, NATO's naval forces conducted a wide range of missions in support of the effort to overthrow the Gaddafi regime. Surface ships and submarines engaged targets ashore with sea-launched strike aircraft, missiles, and gunfire support. Ships also provided afloat-based ISR, interdicted Libyan regime forces attempting to resupply and maneuver from the sea, cleared regime sea mines, and protected humanitarian shipping supporting the insurgents. The potential contributions of seapower in a UW campaign are not limited to intervening navies. In 2012, various websites discussed the formation of a "Free Syrian Navy," and a social media campaign requested donations of fishing boats and other small craft with armor plating and heavy weapons to take on Syrian patrol boats and stop incoming weapons shipments. There is little evidence this nascent naval force was ever used for anything beyond smuggling supplies to rebel forces.

Obviously, the introduction of general purpose forces into an UW campaign signals a significant escalation of U.S. involvement and eliminates any chance at non-attribution if a covert regime change is desired. However, the argument in *Army Special Operations Forces Unconventional Warfare* (FM 3-05.130) that "the strengths of conventional forces (seizing terrain, destroying property, and winning battles against other conventional armed forces) are largely irrelevant and seldom effective in a UW effort,"[29] may need to be reconsidered. It is certainly true that large maneuver elements run the risk of bogging down into an intractable ground war, as occurred in Iraq. But the employment of discrete air and naval combat power *staged outside the country of concern* may accelerate the downfall of a regime during an UW operation. If executed precisely and carefully, these actions will likely reduce the suffering of the local population, which in turn will bolster support for the operation from the international community. UW is the bread and butter of special operations forces, but the utility of seapower and airpower is important enough to be included in any forthcoming joint UW doctrine.

7 UW ON AUTOPILOT – THE SYRIAN CASE STUDY

"The Syrian war is a stalemate. The rebels lack the organization and weapons to defeat Assad; the regime lacks the loyal manpower to suppress the rebellion. Both sides' external allies... are ready to supply enough money and arms to fuel the stalemate for the foreseeable future." – **Bruce Riedel, former senior CIA analyst**[30]

In the same way that technology and social media fuel the flames of insurgencies, these trends will also be used to wage unconventional warfare. External non-state actors provide financial support, coalesce political shadow governments, and even fight alongside insurgents directly on the battlefield. The "open source" unconventional warfare campaigns that have emerged to support the resistance movement against the Assad regime in Syria demonstrate how non-state actors will fill the gap when nation states hesitate to establish comprehensive UW campaigns. The motivations of the private UW practitioners run the gamut from humanitarianism to profit to ideology.

Syria's civil war began in early 2011 as an outgrowth of the Arab Spring. The "fruition of consciousness," or spark that precipitated mass protests in Syria involved the arrest and torture of a group of school children in Deraa, a small Sunni-populated city near the border with Jordan. Fifteen children were arrested by the security services after painting "The People Demand the Fall of the Regime," a slogan made popular during the Egyptian uprising, on the wall of their playground.

Large scale protests evolved into an armed rebellion and by the middle of 2012, fighting had reached the capital at Damascus and the second city of Aleppo. The regime's air power and reported use of chemical weapons was countered by growing external lethal support to the rebels. As international hue and cry escalated to "do

31

something" to alleviate the suffering of the Syrian people, Gulf Arab countries began sending advanced weaponry, including shoulder-launched anti-aircraft missiles to the increasingly-factionalized resistance. In late 2012, various news sources reported that the Obama Administration had authorized the covert training of Syrian rebels in Jordan earlier in the year. The Department of State also publically recognized and supported the Syrian Opposition Coalition (SOC). Via "implementing partners" (contractors) located on the Turkish border, State's Bureau of Conflict and Stabilization Operations (CSO) and the U.S. Agency for International Development (USAID) have provided supplies and equipment such as vehicles and communications gear to more than 3,000 Syrian activists. To complement this non-lethal support, the U.S. CIA began to arm rebels in the summer of 2013. Videos circulating on the Internet in 2014 showed Syria rebels employing U.S. manufactured BGM-71 TOW anti-tank missiles, though these missiles could have also originated from Saudi or Jordanian armories.

Syrian opposition groups attribute tens of thousands of civilian casualties to Assad's helicopter gunships and air-dropped improvised "barrel bombs." In 2013, as casualties mounted and with reports of chemical weapons use against civilians, high level American and European politicians pressed to escalate Western military action. To break the stalemate, a range of desired operations were considered to include the establishment of a no-fly zone and even air and missile strikes against regime targets. The United States positioned air and sea forces in anticipation of an offensive that spring, but due to significant domestic opposition, never fired a shot. Subsequently, numerous rebel requests for support included calls for the shipment of MANPADs to defeat Assad's airpower. Interestingly, in 2014 the leader of a moderate rebel faction remarked that a no-fly zone would be unnecessary if MANPADS were provided to his forces.

In addition to the uneasy alliance of state-sponsored UW campaigns, private individuals began supporting the resistance, which was by now clearly divided along ideological lines. In one example, a Salafi cleric in Kuwait used his Twitter account to persuade his hard line followers to sell their jewelry, automobiles, and other goods to purchase anti-aircraft missiles, rocket propelled grenades, and other equipment for Syrian rebel fighters.[31] Wealthy Gulf state donors had been contributing to jihadists causes (including al Qaeda) for many years, and Syria presented a more legitimate opportunity to support their fellow Salafists.

Another example of private support to the Syrian rebels was reported by Dion Nissenbaum in the *Wall Street Journal*. In 2013, a group of private American citizens led by former Pentagon Inspector General Joseph E. Schmitz and funded by an undisclosed Saudi prince arranged to provide 70,000 Russian made rifles and 21 million rounds of ammunition to the Free Syrian Army (FSA). The group included legitimate arms dealers registered with the U.S. government who would acquire the weapons in the Ukraine. Mr. Schmitz had also spoken to Erik Prince, founder of the former private security company Blackwater, about providing contracted training for the FSA and Prince was ready and willing to do that (for a price). Although the scheme would have been legal according to U.S. laws, for unknown reasons, the CIA reportedly put the brakes on the operation in the summer for 2013.

The ideological bent of some conflicts leads to another trend that complicates UW efforts; that is, the increasing number of Salafist foreign fighters drawn to war zones. This trend dates back to at least the *Mujadin* effort to eject the Soviets from Afghanistan in the 1980s. Since that war, steady streams of Islamist fighters from dozens of countries including the U.S. and Europe have traveled to wage their own UW efforts couched as *jihad* to support local insurgents in Iraq, Yemen, Libya, Mali, and Syria. Al Qaeda in particular frequently develops a parasitic relationship with revolutionaries in Muslim countries, and attempts to coopt the insurgents for its own goals.

It has been estimated that there are over 1,000 separate insurgent factions fighting against regime elements and their supporters in Syria and that up to 5,000 non-Syrian fighters have joined the conflict. For the sovereign nation militaries and agencies conducting UW, these interlopers can be a blessing, a curse, and most of all, a source of confusion. In some cases the outsiders share the goal of regime change; in others their objective is to bring chaos to the battlefield. The al Nusra Front and Islamic State of Iraq and the Levant (ISIS) are aligned with al Qaeda and arguably the strongest and best-armed resistance groups in Syria, so they have drawn the most external support from jihadists. The groups have stated flatly that their objective is establishing an Islamic state, not a Syrian state, which confounds western countries who struggle to support more moderate rebel elements. The fog of war can be thick in any conflict involving non-combatants (e.g., practically all of them), but open source UW is a free-for-all, chaotic endeavor that becomes difficult to control once the non-state actors wield more power than the participating sovereign nations.

The Syrian conflict illustrates another possible complication of unconventional warfare. As previously discussed, a UW campaign, when properly executed, can hasten the downfall of a regime, and reduce the overall casualties and destructiveness of a civil war. In the case of Syria though, an incomplete UW campaign has likely done just the opposite, allowing casualties to build on both sides, while giving just enough hope and support to allow the insurgents to continue fighting indefinitely.

8 CONCLUSION

"... there is no such thing as a local problem anymore ... everything in the world is connected ..." – **Admiral Bill McRaven, Commander, United States Special Operations Command**

Overthrowing a hostile government is a major policy decision with the potential for significant blowback and clearly not an appropriate course of action against all rogue states. The potential for negative unintended consequences of deposing a regime or supporting an insurgent force cannot be overstated. Diplomacy, sanctions, and other external pressure should be given ample time and space to produce the desired effects and alter the regime's objectionable behavior before a regime change campaign is initiated. But when the a western power chooses to undertake such an effort, UW can be a viable and cost-effective method to execute regime change, especially in an era in which large scale military interventions are politically unpopular and operationally unfeasible due to shrinking force structure. The U.S. military and other government agencies involved in UW should be appropriately trained and equipped to conduct these operations in modern, urbanized countries. These campaigns require extensive interagency coordination from the early planning stages through execution. As with any type of war, unity of effort is essential in UW. Because the Department of Defense is likely to provide the preponderance of capabilities in a UW campaign, strong consideration should be given to subordinating other agency elements under the military during an UW effort in order to achieve a more harmonious operation. Moreover, to stay ahead of a regime's decision cycle, agility and freedom to improvise are desirable in UW efforts. Although top down planning and direction is required, authorities to conduct virtual UW campaigns must be pushed to the lowest level possible. Importantly, the increasing trend of non-state actors waging their own concurrent "open-source" UW campaigns will require state-sponsored forces to choose their partners carefully in order to ensure that end state objectives are not derailed.

Dictatorial regimes running amok will remain a national security problem occasionally resulting in the execution of forceful military campaigns for their removal. "In the end, UW should be understood by policy makers, strategists and campaign planners as a strategic option for the U.S. requiring long term preparation to maximize the potential effectiveness."[32] Demographic trends, rapid technological changes, and a creative, adaptive enemy will drive new and innovative UW approaches. An evolution of interagency doctrine and experimentation with new operational concepts and force structures will be required to keep up with the rapidly changing landscape of insurgency and revolution. Moreover, whole-of-government cooperation, flexible authorities, an understanding of emerging technology, and non-traditional partners will be necessary to successfully execute future regime change campaigns.

9 A SELECTION OF TWENTY-FIRST CENTURY UW EFFORTS*

The below operations represent the spectrum of UW participants from independent actors to nation states and demonstrate a variety of outcomes including a rapidly deposed regime and prolonged civil war.

Dates: 1997 - Present
Operation Name: Free Burma Rangers
Location: Myanmar
Affected Regime: Myanmar's Junta
Participants: Private organization
Description: Former U.S. Special Forces operator has led an independent humanitarian organization that provides ethnic resistance forces medical and reconnaissance training.

Dates: 7 October – 26 November 2001
Operation Name: Enduring Freedom
Location: Afghanistan
Affected Regime: Taliban
Participants: U.S., U.K
Description: U.S. and allies supported Northern Alliance fighters to quickly displace Taliban from Afghanistan. Long-term insurgency against nascent government ensued.

Dates: March-April 2003
Operation Name: Viking Hammer
Location: Northern Iraq
Affected Regime: Saddam Hussein
Participants: U.S.
Description: U.S. Special Forces and CIA assisted Kurdish *Peshmerga* guerrillas in holding the Northern Front against regime forces and taking the key oil city of Kirkuk.

Dates: ~2002 - Present
Location: Afghanistan
Affected Regime: Hamid Karzai
Participants: Pakistan's Inter-Services Intelligence Agency (ISI)
Description: Pakistan's ISI has reportedly provided safe haven, arms, and expertise to the Taliban fighting in Afghanistan.

Dates: 2004 - Present
Location: Yemen
Affected Regime: Ali Abdullah Saleh
Participants: Iran/Hezbollah
Description: Iran's Revolutionary Guard and Hezbollah have been accused of providing lethal aid and training support to northern Houthi insurgents against President Ali Abdullah Saleh and Yemen's subsequent leadership.

Dates: 2004 - 2011
Location: Iraq
Affected Regime: Various
Participants: Iranian Revolutionary Guard Force/Hezbollah
Description: Iran's Revolutionary Guard and Hezbollah have been accused of providing social, economic, and lethal aid to Shia insurgents, including advanced explosively formed penetrators (EFPs), which are deadly to modern armored vehicles.

Dates: 2007 - Present
Location: North Korea
Affected Regime: Kim Jong-Un
Participants: North Korea Strategy Center
Description: A group of North Korean Defectors has smuggled thousands of USB media sticks, DVDs, and radios into North Korea with foreign movies, documentaries, and offline versions of Wikipedia to inform DPRK citizens of the outside world with the ultimate goal of overthrowing the Kim regime from within.

Dates: Unknown – 2010?
Location: Somalia
Affected Regime: Somalia Transitional Federal Government
Participants: Eritrea
Description: The United Nations accused the Eritrean government of supplying training, financial support and weapons to armed groups in Somalia, to include al Qaeda-aligned al Shabaab.

Dates: 19 March – October 2011
Operation Name: Odyssey Dawn/Unified Protector
Location: Libya
Affected Regime: Muammar Gadhafi
Participants: U.S., NATO, Qatar, UAE, foreign fighters
Description: U.S.-led/NATO-supported operation began as humanitarian action and transitioned to full-fledged UW campaign to overthrow regime. The operation ended when Gadhafi's convoy was targeted by a U.S. drone strike and French fighter aircraft allowing Gadhafi to be subsequently executed by rebel forces.

Dates: October 2011-Present
Location: Syria
Affected Regime: Bashar al-Assad
Participants: U.S., Qatar, Saudi Arabia, foreign fighters
Description: Gulf Countries reportedly began shipping arms to Syrian rebels in the fall of 2011. U.S. began training rebels in 2012 and arming them in 2013. Fighting continues.

Dates: January – April 2012
Location: Northern Mali
Affected Regime: Coup leader Amadou Sanogo
Participants: Al Qaeda, Ansar Dine, National Movement for the Liberation of Azawad (MNLA), Movement for Oneness and Jihad in West Africa (MUJWA)
Description: Various Tuareg tribes took over large swaths of

Northern Mali supported by Islamic extremists and supplied by weapons from the Libyan conflict. In particular, MUJWA was reportedly aligned and supported by al Qaeda in the Islamic Maghreb. Rebel advances were thwarted short of Bamako in January 2013 when Western military forces led by France came to the defense of the Malian government.

Dates: Spring 2014 - Present
Location: Ukraine
Affected Regime: Acting President Oleksandr Valentynovych Turchynov
Participants: Ukraine, Russia, local police forces, militias
Description: Ukrainian officials allege the presence of Russian special forces troops deployed in Slavyansk and Kramatorsk instigating unrest with pro-Russian separatists militias.

*Information for this list was compiled from various sources. Due to the clandestine nature of most of UW efforts, exact dates, participants, and details of these campaigns are difficult to determine with any accuracy.

BIBLIOGRAPHY

Army Special Operations Forces Unconventional Warfare (FM 3-05.130). Headquarters, Department of the Army, 30 September 2008.

Byrne, Malcolm. *Mohammad Mosaddeq and the 1953 Coup in Iran.* Syracuse, NY: Syracuse University Press, 2004.

"Democracy Index 2011." *Economists Intelligence Unit.* n.d. http://www.eiu.com/public/topical_report.aspx?campaignid =DemocracyIndex2011 (accessed February 18, 2012).

Grdovic, Mark. "Developing a Common Understanding of Unconventional Warfare." *Joint Forces Quarterly*, 2nd Quarter 2010: 136-138.

Greenberg, Andy. "Web Vigilantes." *Forbes Magazine*, January 16, 2012: 36-40.

Haass, Richard N. "Regime Change and Its Limits." *Foreign Affairs*, August July/August 2005: 66-78.

Hartman, Major Scott A. "Airpower Support to Unconventional Warfare." *Masters Thesis.* Fort Leavenworth, Kansas: U.S. Army Command and General Staff College, 2009.

Hosenball, Mark. *Congress secretly approves U.S. weapons flow to 'moderate' Syrian rebels.* January 27, 2014. http://www.reuters.com/article/2014/01/27/us-usa-syria-rebels-idUSBREA0Q1S320140127 (accessed 2014).

Hudson, John. *Islamists Auction Off Cars to Buy Heat Seeking Missiles for Syrian Rebels.* June 27, 2013. http://thecable.foreignpolicy.com/posts/2013/06/27/islami sts_auction_off_cars_to_buy_heat_seeking_missiles_for_syri an_rebels.

Leyne, Jon. *Egypt: Cairo's Tahrir Square fills with protesters.* July 8, 2011. http://www.bbc.co.uk/news/world-middle-east-14075493 (accessed February 26, 2012).

Maxwell, David S. "Why Does Special Forces Train and Educate for Unconventional Warfare?" *Small Wars Journal.* April 21, 2010. http://smallwarsjournal.com/blog/journal/docs-temp/421-maxwell.pdf (accessed January 20, 2012).

Morozov, Evgeny. "Bugger Off - Spying Online Is Perilous and Unnecessary." *Boston Review.Net.* October 2011. http://www.bostonreview.net/BR36.5/evgeny_morozov_internet_spying_privacy.php (accessed January 27, 2012).

Nissenbaum, Dion. "Private U.S. Group Sought To Arm Syrian Rebels." *The Wall Street Journal.* May 19, 2014.

Nelson, Jeff. *Discussions with author on unconventional warfare* (2013).

Paddock, Alfred H. *Psychological and Unconventional Warfare, 1941-1952: Origins of a Special Warfare Capability for the U.S. Army.* Thesis, Carisle, Pennyslvania: US Army War College, 1979.

Petit, Brian. "Social Media and UW." *U.S.Army John F. Kennedy Special Warfare Center and School Special Warfare Magazine.* April 2012. http://www.soc.mil/swcs/SWmag/archive/SW2502/SW2502SocialMediaAndUW.html (accessed April 28, 2013).

Rubenfeld, Samuel. "Treasury Says Libyan Sanctions Blocked $30 Billion." *Wall Street Journal Online.* February 28, 2011. http://blogs.wsj.com/corruption-currents/2011/02/28/treasury-says-libyan-sanctions-blocked-30-billion/ (accessed February 29, 2012).Sorenson, John L., and David K. Pack. *Applied Analysis of Unconventional Warfare.* China Lake, CA: US Ordnance Naval Test Station, April 1964.

Staniland, Paul. "Cities on Fire: Social Mobilization, State Policy, and Urban Insurgency." *Comparative Political Studies* (Sage Publications), no. 43 (June 2010): 1623-1649.

Taber, Robert. *War of the Flea: The Classic Study of Guerrilla Warfare.* New York: Potomac Books, 2002.

The Joint Operational Environment: The World Through 2030 and Beyond. Coordination Draft, United States Joint Forces Command, May 2007.

Titlow, John Paul. *How Syrian Protesters Are Using the iPhone to Fuel an Uprising.* November 18, 2011. http://www.readwriteweb.com/archives/how_syrian_protest ers_are_using_the_iphone_to_fuel.php (accessed February 27, 2012).

NOTES

[1] (Haass July/August 2005)
[2] (Nelson 2013)
[3] (Grdovic 2010)
[4] (Haass July/August 2005)
[5] (Nelson 2013)
[6] (Democracy Index 2011 n.d.)
[7] A more extensive discussion on political and military considerations required for a UW campaign can be found in *Army Special Operations Forces Unconventional Warfare* (FM 3-05.130).
[8] (Maxwell 2010), 4.
[9] (Staniland 2010), 1627.
[10] Ibid, 1630.
[11] (Leyne 2011)
[12] (Haass July/August 2005)
[13] (Nelson 2013)
[14] (Sorenson and Pack April 1964)
[15] (Byrne 2004)
[16] (Paddock 1979)
[17] (Staniland 2010), 1624.
[18] (The Joint Operational Environment: The World Through 2030 and Beyond) May 2007.
[19] (Rubenfeld 2011)
[20] (Taber 2002)
[21] (Titlow 2011)
[22] Ibid.
[23] (Petit 2012)
[24] (Morozov 2011)
[25] (Petit 2012)
[26] (Greenberg 2012)
[27] (Hartman 2009)
[28] Ibid, 14.
[29] (Army Special Operations Forces Unconventional Warfare (FM 3-05.130) 30 September 2008)
[29] (Hosenball)
[31] (Hudson 2013)
[32] (Maxwell 2010), 7.

ABOUT THE AUTHOR

Christopher Rawley, a native Texan, has spent the better half of his professional career as a naval officer in service with special operations and expeditionary units. While assigned to Joint Special Operations Command, Special Operations Command Central, Special Operations Command South, Special Operations Command Africa, and a number of other organizations, he has deployed to the Western Pacific, Arabian Gulf, Afghanistan, Iraq, and Africa.

The opinions and views expressed in this publication are those of the author alone and are presented in his personal capacity. They do not necessarily represent the views of U.S. Department of Defense, the U.S. Navy, or any other government agency.